M000167523

When Crisis Hits

Where to Turn When Life Falls Apart

C. John Miller

New Growth Press

newgrowthpress.com

New Growth Press, Greensboro, NC 27404
newgrowthpress.com

Cover Design: Tandem Creative, Tom Temple,
tandemcreative.net

Typesetting: Lisa Parnell, lparnell.com

ISBN-10: 1-936768-48-8
ISBN-13: 978-1-936768-48-6

        Library of Congress Cataloging-in-Publication Data
Miller, C. John.
  When crisis hits : where to turn when life falls apart / C. John
Miller.
      p. cm.
  Includes bibliographical references.
  ISBN 978-1-936768-48-6 (alk. paper)
  1. Suffering—Religious aspects—Christianity. 2. Consolation.
3. Spirituality. I. Title.
  BV4909.M495 2011
  248.8'6—dc23

                                          2011043177

Printed in India
27 26 25 24 23 22 21 20   8 9 10 11 12

I was resting at home after a trip to the hospital when I heard that the stock market was crashing. I turned on the television and, from my bed, I could see—and almost feel—the gut-wrenching panic among the men and women on the New York Stock Exchange floor. At the end of the day the market was still on a roaring downhill slide. The trustworthy elements in the world of finance had disappeared and the irrational had taken over.

I was especially sensitive to the issue of failed trust that day because just two weeks before I was diagnosed as having an aggressive lymphoma cancer. The news was so shocking that it was hard to take it into my mind. You go for a routine examination and . . .

I don't think it's possible to go through a crisis like the stock market slide or a cancer diagnosis without feeling that somebody is trying to speak some kind of special message meant for you. When the bottom falls out of your investments or your family or your health, you can't escape the insistent question, What can you really trust in anyway?

At such critical times I have learned that you either trust in yourself and human supports or you trust in God.

Ralph Waldo Emerson, a famous American philosopher, opted for trusting himself. In his essay "On Self-Reliance," he said, "Trust thyself; every heart vibrates to that iron string." If all Emerson meant was to have confidence in your own training and abilities, fine. He was only saying, "Know what you can do and do it without fear. Don't lose your nerve."

But Emerson was saying a lot more than that. He meant that the potential for solving all your problems lies within yourself. That's a very attractive idea. We like to be told that we have great human potential and that there is no difficulty we cannot overcome if we tap the resources in ourselves. Certainly there is a germ of truth in this idea. Each of us does have qualities we can draw upon to help us through our crises. But is it really true that we have in ourselves the potential for solving all our problems?

The Limits of Human Potential

Think about it. Can you change a positive test for cancer to negative? When your wife or husband walks out on you, can you win back your spouse by willpower? When your rebellious teenager becomes alienated from you and you fear serious drug involvement, are you really able to find the potential to help him from within yourself?

When life falls apart, we feel deep confusion in the depths of our being. We discover that life is not under our control, and we don't like it at all. Our emotions may shatter no matter how strong we have been. Instead of being able to find unlimited resources within ourselves when the doctor says, "You have cancer," our minds fill with unanswered and painful questions like,

"Why me?"
"What did I do to deserve this?"
"Is there any hope for my future?"
"Do I even have a future?"

The illusion that you have within yourself the potential to cope with any problem can do more to defeat you at your point of crisis than almost anything else.

I once worked for a wealthy businessman, Paul Townsend.* The president of several successful

---

*All names have been changed.

companies, he believed that optimism and self-confidence was all you needed to succeed in life. He shared his views with me every morning when I came to work. The leading idea was always that your goals could be reached by rejecting all negative thinking and believing that you could accomplish anything in business and life.

He would often complete these little training sessions by reminding me, "Remember, don't be negative; you can do anything you want for the future." I can still remember him standing there. He was already past sixty-five and his graying hair was thinning, but his figure was trim, his manner vigorous, and his self-assurance absolute. He seemed to be his own best advertisement for his philosophy of success in business and ultimately in life.

A winner all the way, he had successfully pioneered various kinds of innovations in company management styles and had been for years a leading philanthropist. As my employer, he treated me well and allowed me time from my job to work on my doctorate at a nearby university.

But one day he had his own personal crisis where his world fell apart. He had neglected to watch certain investments that supported the foundation I worked for. A large sum of money was lost, probably through the mismanagement of others. But Paul was the man in charge, and he believed he should have watched these investments more closely. He felt intense self-condemnation and guilt. Soon after, he had a stroke.

When he returned to his work after several weeks, our roles were almost reversed. The first time I went to his office to encourage him, he was sitting behind his desk looking old and exhausted. The glint in his blue eyes was gone; his face looked gray. At first I thought his physical appearance was entirely due to the stroke. But it soon became clear that, although he had made considerable progress in recovering from the stroke, the real problem was that he was filled with fears and negative thoughts. It was as if the bottom had fallen out of his life and nothing could help him. Life for him had become unsafe, threatening.

To help him, I tried some plain talk: "Look, Mr. Townsend. You need to shift your faith from yourself and your abilities. I believe it will make a real difference if you put your trust in God and in Christ, not in yourself."

He began to ask me questions, something he had never done before. The help he began to receive didn't have much to do with me. God was beginning to speak to him, and tough-minded and independent as he was, Paul listened to what was said. From all I could tell he found a release in what I told him.

Pain Leads to Peace

"God whispers to us in our pleasures," wrote C. S. Lewis, noted English author, ". . . but shouts to us in our pain."[1]

I believe this is what happens to all of us when we come up against our brick walls and we're left standing there with hurt and despair. God speaks to us at such times in megatons, and a whole new way of life can begin for us, one with wonderful promise for learning things that are beautiful beyond our dreams. If we listen to him, we can find purpose and joy in life—even at the toughest of times—that simply transcend description. I know about this because I have found it for myself. It does not mean there are no more crises or that sorrows or pains disappear like magic. No, you still go through the experiences of life. You may still fear death in the night or keenly regret your divorce, but you do not go alone any longer.

Often our sufferings help us to see that our key human values have been confused and debased. In our pain we might sense that we have loved money more than God, and what really makes us happiest is basking in the glory of our career triumphs. Or we might sense that the highest desires in us have been neglected while we have sought our own comfort.

By themselves, sufferings don't bring you to this new kind of confidence in God. When I had my initial encounter with cancer, I learned that the pain of the situation can open you to listen to God, but in and of itself it can also leave you in despair. As I was lying on my hospital bed, God made it clear to me that he wanted me to undergo a deep change within myself. He wanted me to shift my whole confidence from myself to him. It did not come to me as a loud demand from God, but as a quiet pressure of love.

You might think that it would have been natural for me to do what God wanted—just to trust him all the way at that point. After all, what choice did I have? The lymphoma was massive, overwhelming the kidneys, which had ceased to function. Unless the kidneys started working again, I would not be able to take the chemotherapy necessary to shrink my tumor and save my life. The doctors knew I had a weakened heart and were unsure whether it could handle the strain of the kidney failure and the growing cancer. But the temptation for me was to be overwhelmed by fear and passively give up the fight, even perhaps turning away from God to lapse into numbness, self-pity, and fear.

Mercifully, I felt instead a gentle drawing away from myself toward reliance on God. This shift in my confidence came to me through the prayers of the many people who were asking God to deliver me. As they prayed, I was able to put myself entirely in God's hands. Even as I spent four days in the Coronary Care Unit hooked up to life-support systems, I experienced peace amid waves of weakness.

A wonderful physical recovery followed. While many people prayed, my kidneys started functioning, and a few hours after exploratory surgery the doctors were able to give me chemotherapy. But the biggest change was in my deepened knowledge that I was now entirely in the hands of God and could trust him fully in circumstances which were entirely out of my control.

Why Do I Resist God?

But my experiences raise a key question: why do I resist putting my full confidence in God? What makes us humans so instinctively want to trust in ourselves instead of him? Exploring the unpopular concept of sin can help answer these questions. Psychiatrist Karl Menninger writes in his book, *Whatever Became of Sin?*, that there is so much despair in our time because we have lost the word "sin" from our vocabulary and therefore cannot understand ourselves.

He says that sin has in it "a breaking away from God and from the rest of humanity." Breaking away from God is a quality of sin; it means that we do not want him to rule over us. Menninger adds, "Sin has a willful, defiant or disloyal quality: someone is defied or offended or hurt."[2]

The Bible, in explaining the concept more fully, says that sin is a radical rejection of God's rule over our lives. As such, sin is an act of treason by the created human being committed against his

Creator. The Bible explains that God made each of us with unique dignity and freedom in his image. But as his creatures we are also totally dependent on him for the gift of life, our health, our jobs, the food we eat, the clothing we wear, the water we drink, and even the air we breathe. But we express our "breaking away from God" by acting as though his good gifts were our own possessions. We live for the gifts, but reject the Giver (Romans 1:25). We act as though God was our "heavenly bellhop," duty bound to come instantly when we call for him to meet our needs. Instead of worshipping God and having him at the center of our world, we put ourselves and our desires at the center of our lives and expect God to do what we ask.

You can see how this works in our world. We see some people driven by power and reputation. Some of them are cocky and cruel, and in their greed will crush anyone to get ahead. Others are nice, decent types who neglect their families to win a senior vice-presidency, make another million, or establish an enviable reputation. One such "winner" reported that he gained a high position in his firm, but in the process lost his family and self-respect. Others seek to build an independent life by good deeds and public service.

Sin makes us our own worst enemy and hides from us our true welfare. For without submission to God our deepest longings remain unmet. God designed us to find our security in living under his loving control and care. St. Augustine had it right when he prayed to God, "You have created us for yourself, and we are restless until we find our rest in you."

We believed that relationships or money or a successful career could satisfy us. When these things fail to satisfy and begin to disappear, God gently fills our minds with probing questions such as these:

- How do I switch my confidence from myself to him?
- Can I really trust my future to him when I feel shaken by sickness?
  - By the loss of my job?
  - By family problems?
- Can I really have a personal relationship with a God I can't even see?

The First Step

The Bible is very clear about how to have a personal relationship with God. But there is a very difficult first step. It is not an easy one for anyone to take. It is simply this: you cannot get to know God unless you are first willing to listen to him.

Naturally though, we are all poor listeners. I remember talking with a senior executive of a high tech firm on a plane trip. He told me how successful his company had been the previous year. He totally believed in the power of self-confidence and the Emersonian idea of "trust thyself."

I tried to disagree with his outlook. But he had quick replies to everything I said. It was obvious that he was accustomed to being in control of any meeting in which conflicting points of view were expressed. He had a way of coming out right, no matter what I suggested. He was hearing my words and arguing with me, but he didn't trouble himself to understand the ideas. It became a frustrating conversation for me because he wasn't really listening.

Finally, I blurted out, "Look, I'm sorry, but I don't think you have been listening to what I'm trying to say."

There was a moment of silence. I had the uncomfortable feeling that nobody had ever talked this way to him. Would he be offended? He obviously was shocked. But to my surprise, he said quietly, "All right, what do you think is wrong with us and what's the answer?"

"In our country we need a return to God," I told him. "I'm thinking of leaders like you and me. We are proud men, and we need to repent, really humble ourselves before God. We need to get rid of our self-sufficiency and let God take over our lives."

Now he was obviously listening. Then to my astonishment, he replied thoughtfully, "It makes sense, what you are saying. Humbling ourselves before God—I think I agree with you that is our real need."

A mysterious thing began to happen as we continued to talk. He was not only listening to me; he was beginning to listen to God. It was clear that God was speaking to him. My words about not listening had arrested his attention, but God was *keeping* his attention.

Of course, you do not have to be an executive on an airplane to start listening to God. God wants you to hear in your heart what he says about himself, whoever you are and wherever you are, right now. It is an urgent issue. The Bible is his written Word and it tells you that he is both holy and compassionate. He also knows the inmost depths of your motives and longings. Though he is very compassionate, he is holy and insists on you becoming honest about yourself.

He wants you to admit that you are a sinner and that your efforts to control your own life are a radical defiance of his will. Isaiah 53:6 says, "We all, like sheep, have gone astray, each of us has turned to his own way . . . ." Because God knows we are trapped in our own willful ways he sent his own Son, Jesus, as an atoning sacrifice for us. Isaiah 53:6 concludes, "and the LORD has laid on him [Jesus] the iniquity of us all." This is the greatest act of love in all history: the Son of God became man and died on the cross to bring eternal life to all who believe.

What Does Believing in God Mean?

Believing! That brings us right back to our beginning question about who we trust in—ourselves or

God. We must choose between believing in our own powers to deliver us, or believing in God exclusively.

You may think, *Yes, I will trust in God, but I must do my part too. I must become more religious, going to church or synagogue, doing good works, and trying to live a better life.*

I held this point of view myself as a young man of twenty. To get near to God, I reformed a number of my habits and became faithful in religious activities. But I found it didn't actually bring me any nearer to God. Why? Because my attempts at self-improvement didn't really deal with my pride. I hadn't humbled my heart before God. I still wanted control of my life and lived for my own glory, not God's. As I prayed I was talking to God, but I wasn't listening to him. An older Christian helped me by telling me, "Believing is the very opposite of trying harder to be good or to earn a relationship with God. It is personally trusting in Christ and receiving him into your life as your Lord and Savior."

Believing in the biblical sense also has in it an honesty—a willingness to face up to the facts about yourself and how you have offended God by trying to run your own life independently of him. For some people it might mean an honest confession that they have loved money and power more than God. For others it would mean admitting that they have been sold out to maximizing physical pleasure, and for yet others it would be acknowledging the thrill of conquest through an intensely competitive business or professional style. For still others it would be repenting of trying to build a family life according to their own will and way. But for everyone, at bottom, it would come down to the humbling acknowledgment, "I have offended God by trying to run my own life without him."

Are you ready to believe? Believe that you are in peril because you have sinned against a holy God. But also believe that God loves you unconditionally and sent his only Son to die for you—while you were still bent on living without him. Trust that the holy Father gave his perfect Son to take away all your condemnation and give you eternal life.

Such faith is more than a good feeling about believing. It is simply receiving Christ. If you receive Christ, you have living faith in him. But your peril without Christ is great. You are in the hands of the living God, and you must take seriously his warning to flee from eternal judgment. Therefore pray something like this: *God, I humble my proud heart and admit that I have tried to control my own life, as though I were my own god. Please forgive me. I now put my trust in Jesus, who died to take away my sins. I surrender to him as the Lord of all my life.*

Facing the Future

Does this new relationship mean that you will have no more fears about the future, your health, lost investments, or family problems?

I am writing this in a very beautiful setting. It is early winter, and I am looking out the window of my study at the large Japanese cherry tree that dominates our backyard. In the spring it is radiant with white buds; in the early winter it is still lovely with the small, bright cherries that make it look like a Christmas decoration. My room is light and airy and I am sitting in a pool of sunshine. I feel that all this beauty is a gift of God to me and a sign of his care. But I am also describing to you my battleground. It is here that I live, eat, work, and recover from chemotherapy. Here I fight for my life against cancer and the fears that go with it. I do so with all my heart and courage because I am filled with confidence in Christ, not in my own powers and strength. He is the one who has made me a victor, not a victim, and a fighter, not a quitter.

Certainly we may struggle with some fears all of our days. The thought of death sometimes comes to me at night when I am taking chemotherapy in the hospital. I can admit that the fear is real, take it to my friend Jesus, and ask him to take it away. As I deepen in honesty with him, his presence with me grows ever stronger. There is nothing sweeter and purer than to know Christ is with me, whether my life is long or short. This is a tremendous release from the multitude of pressures I feel as I travel to and from the hospital. Now I can take my deepest fears to him, grow in my confidence in his control of my destiny, and find my security in him. I can find in his friendship the most important thing in life—the satisfying of my deepest longing to be loved unconditionally by someone who fully understands me.

Open your own life to Christ, and he will live inside you. Find in him your unlimited resources for coping with even the most overwhelming problems of life—the crises that we all eventually have to face. Put all your confidence in Christ alone to make you a victor.

Endnotes

1. C. S. Lewis, *The Problem of Pain* (New York: HarperCollins, 2001), 91.

2. Karl Menninger, *Whatever Became of Sin?* (New York: Bantam Books, 1988), 19.

Simple, Quick, Biblical

Advice on Complicated Counseling Issues
for Pastors, Counselors, and Individuals

MINIBOOK
CATEGORIES

- Personal Change
- Marriage & Parenting
- Medical & Psychiatric Issues

- Women's Issues
- Singles
- Military

USE YOURSELF I GIVE TO A FRIEND I DISPLAY IN YOUR CHURCH OR MINISTRY

New Growth Press

Go to **www.newgrowthpress.com** or call **336.378.7775** to
purchase individual minibooks or the entire collection.
Durable acrylic display stands are also available to house
the minibook collection.